LETTERS
TO A
TEEN-AGE
SON

BOOKS BY HENRY GREGOR FELSEN

LETTERS TO A TEEN-AGE SON

by Henry Gregor Felsen

DODD, MEAD & COMPANY NEW YORK

TO

LANCE CORPORAL

DANIEL FELSEN,

USMC

CONTENTS

LETTERS
TO A
TEEN-AGE
SON

FOREWORD:
NOTES TO A
GROWING BOY

IT IS the middle of a May morning in West Des Moines, Iowa. On this pleasant spring day I am in my study at home, looking out of the window at golfers on the course across the street. You are in school. No matter what is going on in the classroom, I imagine you are also looking out of a window, probably thinking about cars. I am thinking about you, and how to reach you.

Like most fathers, I have hoarded up a vast sum of advice which I am constantly trying to transfer to your account, and which you—like most children—insist be retained in my name. Yet there are times when you want to talk to me about yourself and your life, and actively seek my opinion and advice.

My problem, when you come to me, is not knowing when to quit. When you ask me for a specific, limited opinion on one subject, I usually respond with an endless lecture that exhausts and bores you, and usually fails to answer your question. This happens because our moments of rapport are few and far between. When they come I try to make too much of them, and thereby make too little. I try too hard because our watches, so to speak, are not synchronized. At my age sixty minutes flash by like sixty seconds; at your age they creep past like sixty hours.

You do not have many years left under my roof, and I am unwilling, in the time we have left together, to depend on chance moments of closeness to talk to you. Yet I have little faith in planned lectures delivered at my convenience, or in contrived discussions which often break down into pointless arguments.

How *can* I reach you?

Sitting here this May morning watching the golfers, while you doze in school dreaming of cars, I think I have found the answer. I am by profession and nature a writer. You are by training and nature a boy who loves to read. I can write what I cannot say. You will read what you do not have the patience to hear. I believe we can meet more intimately as writer and reader than we ever could as father and son.

The written word offers freedom to me and protection to you. I can, without being rushed by your impatience, say fully what I want you to hear. You can, at your own need and convenience, seek my opinions in whatever privacy of person, moment or emotion you require.

Somehow, I find myself at this moment thinking of my father. How I wish he were alive, so I could tell him I understand at last why he so often —and so fruitlessly—tried to sit down and talk to me when I was a boy. Not that I would agree with him. Our generations and natures were too far apart for agreement, and still would be. But I wish he could know that I understand his need, as my father, to subject his intimate feelings and treasured philosophies to my shallow, uncomprehending, scornful and supercilious inspection.

Today I sit where my father sat, and where his father—and his father's father—sat, and I have you for a son, and my heart is filled with the same need to reach you with my feelings, my lessons learned and my philosophies. For I too have the father's instinct, duty and desire to care for you in my home while you are small, and to teach you to survive in the world when you are grown.

I use the word survive, but I do not mean it in its grim, limited, head-just-above-the-water sense. By survive, I mean your ability to live to the full the wonderful human life that is yours.

I mean your vocational survival in a world where every opportunity is every day more fiercely contested.

I mean your cultural survival in a society which besieges your young mind on all sides with cheap entertainments, cheap diversions and cheap philosophies.

I mean your moral survival in a century which mass-produces vulgar ideals, vulgar goals and vulgar satisfactions.

I mean what amounts to your sexual survival as a man who will marry a woman and reproduce your kind in a stable, satisfying family situation —immune to the destructive definition of sex as a brief physical contact between any male and any female.

We live in a century and a country that offer unlimited opportunities for human growth, experience and happiness. You are free to be anything you are capable of being, and the list is long. You are free to live where and how you desire, and the land is wide. You are free to choose your occupation, your religion, your morals and your mate. Further, the entire resources of our society are available to help you become as fine a man as is in your power and ability.

It was not always so, nor is it everywhere now true. There are boys who still grow to manhood under the watchful eyes of a tribe or state or dogma that marks out the narrow paths they must travel, prescribes the narrow thoughts they must think and imposes on them the restricted lives they must lead and the tasks they must perform.

But sadder than these slaves of tribe or state are the slaves of this free world, who shuffle through life with their unyoked necks bowed, and their unchained wrists pressed together.

The possible tragedy of your life is not that you might fail to become healthy, wealthy and wise, but that, through lack of interest, curiosity or initiative, you apprentice yourself to half the man you could be.

I will give you two examples out of your own life to show what I mean by these words.

You are bursting with the desire to be "grown-up." To you, that means reaching an age where you can do whatever you want to. But it is now, and not after you have grown up, that you face the most important responsibilities of your entire life. For it is now, perhaps more than at any other time, that it is in your power to decide how you will live in the future.

There is something cruel and unfair about the fact that, at your tender age, you may already have limited your future. You hated algebra, saw no reason why you had to excel in it, and, grinding out the work with half a heart, got a low grade. So . . . ?

So, in your school, that eliminates you from going on to take geometry, which in turn shuts off the entire future study of math. The future careers which you have erased from your slate with one poor grade would fill a book. Perhaps, somewhere among the lost, is your "right" future.

It isn't that I want you to be an engineer or a scientist. I want you to be whatever you are happy being, whether it be a guide, mechanic, teacher, doctor, artist or race driver. What I do care about now is that you do your best to *keep open* every possible path to your future, so you can walk the one of your choice. And it is now, while you are too young to know which road to the future is yours, that you are "old enough" to close off a thousand possible avenues to life.

I know you well. So far your victories outnumber your defeats. But, in your world, victories are taken for granted, and defeats are shattering. Sometimes I wonder which of us is the more grown up, when I realize that, as a man, I can make more mistakes than you without penalty, I am allowed more failures, I find more tolerance for my weaknesses and inabilities. Life demands much more perfection from you, the child, than it asks of me, the man.

That was a rather obvious example of how your present behavior and attitudes are, at this very moment, shaping your future life. Let's look at another, not quite so obvious, but perhaps more important example.

It has been said that listening to music over a poor sound system can give you a "tin ear," incapable of appreciating a higher fidelity of sound reproduction. I am concerned that your exposure to vulgar and narrow outlooks on life now, will give you a "tin soul."

This is why I have been critical of your addiction to various fads that have come and gone. No fad you ever followed was good or evil as such, whether it was how high you wore your hair or how low you wore your pants. But to obey a fad blindly is to let the mob do your thinking for you. And if you get in the habit of letting others dictate your mode of dress, action and speech now, you will find it difficult, perhaps impossible, to think and act for yourself when you are older. Or you may not have the courage to do so. At your age the mob demands hair. At mine, it demands heads.

The high school custom of beating up another boy whose crime is that he attends a different school produces adults who are conditioned to kill other humans whose crime is that they live in another country, speak a different language or belong to a different race or religion.

I am not telling you to be different from the majority just for the sake of being different. This too is a fad. Whatever you do I want you to do consciously, of your own will, honestly aware of your motives, the satisfactions you seek and the limitations you have imposed upon yourself. This awareness will not always protect you from doing what is foolish, but it will keep you free.

My purpose in writing this little series of letters is not to tell you how to live, but how to be aware of life. I will not pretend that all my analyses are correct, my interpretations flawless or my attitudes wise. Spiritually as well as materially, I can make you heir only to that which I thought worth gaining, in the amount I have been able to retain. More than some men, less than others. I come to you not with a schedule of living to be learned by rote, but with opinions I hope you will honor, even—perhaps *especially*—when your own life and times prove them old-fashioned, deficient and inept.

It has been said that parents, in advising their children, are arming them to fight the wars of the future with the weapons of the past. What I hope to give you here is not a miracle weapon with which to smite all the problems in your life. Rather, I offer something more in the nature of a little pocket knife that can be carried anywhere, in any kind of campaign. A handy little tool that, in the small emergencies, can uncork bottles, open cans, remove splinters, de-hook fish, whittle kindling, snip wire, toast meat, sharpen pencils and turn screws.

For no matter how different your future world might seem from this one, it will be born of these and past times and will, like all children, resemble its ancestors. Even as you resemble me historically, as well as physically.

Today you stand ankle-deep in the nuclear age as I, at your age, stood at that depth in the electronic. And the changes of the next twenty-five years will reduce almost to the status of parlor tricks the miracles of the past twenty-five. But even in a world of fantastic machinery and scientific wonders, what is most ancient in man will remain unchanged, and up-to-date.

The human need for and the essentials of goodness, decency and righteousness are as modern as they are ancient, and no future time will ever turn them into museum pieces.

In your world, and in your children's world too, friends will be treasured for their loyalty, lovers for their constancy, men for their integrity and women for their tenderness. Parents of the future may scan skyways instead of highways for a sign of teen-agers out too late, but the worried looks they exchange will be as old as the caves. And babies, waking from bad dreams in the middle of the future's marvelous night, will still cry for their mothers—though it be by radio from an air-conditioned, sound-engineered nursery.

As I expect your world will in time surpass mine in every physical and moral way, so in time I expect you to surpass me. But as your world must, to become better, learn from the trials and errors of the old, so must you, to surpass me, learn from my trials and errors, my successes and failures, my experiences and my observations.

In a way, these letters represent what I see when I look at you. They might help you find yourself in a crowd.

I will begin with your beginning. We know who you are now, and what kind of boy you have become. But your dimensions are meaningless if measured only by the present fragments of your life. They become meaningful when you know your own history; when you understand the moment to which you trace your individual life.

You are here for reason. You have become with cause. Let us turn to the blueprints of your existence, and establish your identity.

WHY YOU
WERE BORN

When I was a boy and my father criticized me, I often threw him a curve I thought no parent could hit. I would try to knock him off balance by declaring haughtily, "I didn't ask to be born!"

More than once you have said the same thing

to me. But you are wrong. I don't know if I asked to be born, but I know you did. You did more than ask. You clamored for birth. You nagged more to be born than you have teased and tormented for anything else since.

You know that, aside from biological instinct and accidents incident to passion, there are many reasons why people have children. I doubt if any two pairs of parents have ever had exactly the same reasons for wanting a child. And even with the same parents, each child in the family owes his origin to reasons that are uniquely and exclusively his own.

Children are conceived for serious reasons and for silly ones. They are conceived in joy and sorrow. They are conceived to reward and to punish. They are the result of malice aforethought, and of love. They are conceived in the hope of saving shaky marriages and to enrich solid ones. They are conceived with hope and with apprehension. Positive proof of a tiny being alive in the womb may bring tears of happiness and rapture, or of panic and despair.

Some humans believe parenthood their religious or patriotic duty. Others want heirs to inherit fortunes or carry on family names. Some people want children to love, and others want them to exploit. Some women envision babies as living dolls to be played with; others are moved by a compelling instinct to bear, raise, and subordinate their lives to their young. Some men have fathered babies in order to avoid military service, or to "prove" their virility, or for added tax exemptions. And other men have become fathers in a supreme gesture of love and devotion and confidence in their wives.

Why, then, were *you* born?

Your mother and I were married six years before you were born. You weren't born sooner because you didn't ask sooner.

She and I were married at twenty. We were twenty-three before I began earning a living as a writer and we were able to move out of musty furnished rooms and into a modern apartment. We bought furniture. We acquired a car.

When all this happened, my life seemed as full as a life could be. My dreams of love and work had come true. What more could I need to make my life complete? Nothing more. I needed only the same love, the same work, the same life.

Then *somehow*—and I cannot tell you exactly when or how this feeling came—a two-person family was not enough. For the first time in our lives, your mother and I began to know that being together as man and wife was too little to dispel the loneliness; the rooms we two had once filled seemed empty. Although we had achieved everything we hoped for it was not enough. Suddenly, we found we wanted to exchange our precious freedom for deeper and more lasting roots. We had reached the peak of the mountain. Our two-person relationship now had nowhere to go but down.

This need for a child is a strange, mystifying, unsettling urge. It is difficult to describe a yearning for someone who does not exist, a need to subordinate one's life to a small creature unknown and not yet created. For me, the need to be your father was the most solemn, yet stimulating, emotion of all my life.

"To every thing," the Bible says, "there is a season, and a time to every purpose under the heaven: A time to be born, and a time to die; a time to plant, and a time to pluck up that which is planted. . . ."

Your time and your season had arrived. Now you insisted on being born. You demanded life.

How suddenly aware we were of the silences that ached for your cry and the emptiness that could be filled only by you. I—who cared little for babies in general, and less for any that I had happened to encounter—I felt lost, incomplete, and unfulfilled because I did not have one of my own. The one that was you. Even then, I think, I knew it was you as well as I know it today.

Your mother and I needed to have you because our growth as human beings had not halted with marriage. Now we needed you to complete our life, our function, and our love.

Unproductive sex, once the supreme experience, now took on the aspect of an evasive sensual exercise. Our love for each other was not enough. We needed to merge our separate loves into one, and share it jointly with and through you. Only then would we two be one.

I do not know when—or even if—you will become a father, or the circumstances under which fatherhood will take place, if it does. I do not expect your emotional life to duplicate mine. But I hope you will be fortunate enough to be called to fatherhood by a voice as sweet and strong as your own. And in any case, I have a wish for you.

I wish and hope that parenthood will not first come to you as the result of a sexual slip, albeit within the legal bonds of matrimony.

The act of conscious creation brought to me— as it might well bring to you—a moment of sub- lime experience unlike anything I had ever imag- ined, much less known. To miss knowing the difference between sex and the *awareness* of mat- ing is to miss one of life's most perfect, most meaningful moments.

It seemed to me that all my life and the lives of all my ancestors had been lived for the sole pur- pose of culminating in you. In that moment as in no other, I was, as a human being, fulfilled and at peace with my spirit. I felt a tremendous new will to live, yet knew I could die with fewer re- grets. I felt a sense of human love and biological duty at once completely done. And I felt, with some joy and with some terror, the coming change in my life from someone I had been, to someone I was going to be; a change almost as extreme as your change from no one to someone.

All our lives up to and including marriage we

are ourselves as we came into the world, growing older. When we become parents we make the only real qualitative rather than quantitative, change as human beings. The night you were born I ceased being my father's boy and became my son's father. That night I began a new life.

You have always known me in the role of father, and I doubt that you will ever be able to see me as anything else. But some day, perhaps, you will understand that until you brought me the title and duty of parent, I was more boy than man. Some day, perhaps when you become a father, you will know that it was you who made me a man.

WHEN YOU
FALL IN LOVE

I SUPPOSE I would be violating one of fatherhood's oldest traditions if I did not take you aside sooner or later for a man-to-man talk about sex, love, and mating.

If I hesitate, it is not because of any false modesty or embarrassment over speaking on this topic. Rather, I am at a loss as to where to begin, and what to say that will be of any value to you.

The problem is that the so-called facts of life and love are not rules and regulations of conduct, that, like a soldier's general orders, can be committed to memory for once and for all and will cover all sentries and situations equally. What we are dealing with are the facts of one particular life as it develops from childhood to maturity, and what these facts are depends on who and what that person is, and on whom he marries. The facts grow out of life lived together, and are not applied to it like a poultice.

To be arbitrary about it, the facts of life and love as they come into your life can be divided into three related areas. There is sex information, which is mainly biological and mechanical. There is sex education, which includes the emotional factors and relationships. And, finally, there is what I would call sexual comprehension, which is the ability of a man and a woman to live together successfully under one roof as mates, roommates, parents, and partners in the over-all business of being and running a family.

There are two major obstacles in trying to communicate any of these facts—or an awareness of them—to you: one, my own limitations in comprehending and articulating; the other, your limitations in being able to understand what I am trying to say. Even the best information is useless if it is given before you are ready to understand it intellectually and appreciate it emotionally. Thus there are some "facts of life" that you can understand at six, and others that may not make sense to you until you are 60 and a grandfather.

What I am about to tell you is what I am convinced you need to know now.

The other day I passed by the garage, where you and your car-club buddies were working on the ancient jalopy you are restoring to life. As I passed I heard you sounding off about a boy who had been a member of the club and one of your closest friends. The reason for your scorn was that he had deserted the car club in order to go steady with a girl. This, I gathered from your remarks, was in your view not only treasonable but incomprehensible.

As I listened, it struck me that in spite of school sex-information films, racy magazines, earthy novels, and earnest bull sessions, you really do not understand how or why it is necessary for boys to become infatuated with girls or for men to fall in love with women. You seem to have no idea why, being a normal boy, the same thing can, and will, and must happen to you. Unless I can make this seemingly obvious but most subtle matter clear, none of the other facts of life will have much meaning for you.

As of now, you see your future in terms of your present—only more so. Instead of a boy with an old car, you see your future self as a man with a new car, and the time to come as a time when you will be old and independent enough to obtain and enjoy the good things life has to offer.

These good things are, by your present definition, all the good things you want now, and which you are confident you will continue to want in the future. And, just as you cannot imagine ever *not* wanting the things you want now, you cannot imagine ever wanting anything you do not presently want.

And yet, the time is almost at hand when it won't be as much fun to hang around with a crowd of boys as with a crowd of boys and girls.

And not long after that, you will find there is one girl you like to be with and that when you are with her you can do without the rest of the crowd. But even when that time comes, dating and crushes will be only segments of your life. You will flee from the most wonderful girl in the world if she should happen to mention one word about "our" future.

You are very positive that you will never give up the advantages of bachelorhood just to marry some girl. What, marry and have to spend on *furniture* and *dishes* the money that can buy triple-carb manifolds and exhaust headers? Never!

What you want is to escape my nosey interest in your personal affairs, not merely to exchange my nosiness for a wife's. You want to escape your mother's nagging about your manners, clothes, and carelessness, not to exchange it for a wife's.

You are not about to exchange the personal restrictions imposed upon you by your parents for the tougher restrictions imposed by a wife and children.

Never! Not on your life.

It won't be long now, as you see it, before you —fully grown, independent, and free—will live the seemingly ideal life of the mature bachelor. Your life will seem to have reached its most glorious peak.

Your entire existence can be devoted to the pursuit of such studies, pleasures, interests, and projects as appeal to you. You can eat when you are hungry, drink when you are dry.

The variety of your experiences need be limited only by your own impulses and capabilities. You will have dates when you feel like feminine company; you will travel alone when you don't.

You will, I am sure, enjoy to the utmost this period of freedom, this opportunity to do everything, without being burdened by the necessity to do anything. And you no doubt will vow on many a pleasant occasion to continue to live your life at this most perfect level. No other way of life will seem to offer more and demand less.

And yet, somehow there will come a time when you feel you have lived up all the life that single blessedness has to offer. A time when freedom, pleasure, opportunity, lack of responsibility, self-centeredness, and self-indulgence are not, somehow, enough to fill your life.

Then you will feel that there must be a change

in the entire basis of your existence if life is to be more than a repetition of experiences and situations that have begun to pall. A time when your life, to have freshness, challenge, meaning, and satisfaction, must catch up with your growth. A time when you outgrow your adult bachelorhood as you are now outgrowing your childhood.

When, as you have been doing all your life, you outgrow not only your old treasures, haunts, interests, and diversions, but your very self.

Now you will understand that physical desire for a woman is senior in time to—but not the same as—a man's need for a mate. You will recognize that your hungers are not of the body, but of the soul; that the turbulence is not in your loins, but in your heart; that it is not your fiery passions that must be cooled, but your cold life made warm.

Just as in your bachelor days you needed freedom from emotional entanglements and restraints for your life to be full, you will find that your life is now empty and unsatisfactory without them. You will need a wife, just as once, to live a full and normal life, you needed parents.

Even more, for the first time in your life you

will need someone whose existence, welfare, and happiness are more precious to you than your own. Only with her, and only in marriage, can you take the next logical, necessary step in your growth to complete manhood.

Why will you fall in love? Not primarily because of differences between your first and your last sweetheart—not because of things like the brightness of their eyes or their tastes in music.

You will fall in love because you really must; because you need the help of a woman to become your final possible self.

Male and female we are brought into this world. Male and female we grow to maturity. Male and female we can be healthy, wealthy, and wise. But separate, we can never go beyond being male and female.

It is only when a female marries that, via mating and motherhood, she becomes completely and in every way a woman. You, as a male, will fall in love and marry because it is only a woman, in marriage, who can release you from the prison of mere maleness and enable you to become, in every sense of the word, a man and a mature human being.

YOU AND
YOUR MOTHER

WHENEVER a comedian wants to get a laugh and can't think of a sure-fire joke, he can always resort to slipping on a banana peel or remarking that a boy's best friend is his mother. I don't know why that line always draws a laugh, or why I myself have laughed at it, because it is the honest if not so simple truth.

I am sure you know your mother loves you, yet I doubt that you would ever think of including her name on any list of your good friends you might make. As your father, it is conceivable, but unlikely, that I would make the grade. But your mother? Never. The idea just wouldn't occur to you.

The very fact that you are unaware that your mother is the best friend you have in the world is, in itself, conclusive evidence that she is. The most I can be or hope to be is your second best friend. Let me explain.

Several years ago, when I was doing hospital research for a medical-background novel, I had the chance to observe two interns in action. One of them was tall, handsome, outgoing, and very much at ease with everyone he met. He worked his way through the wards with bright smiles, reassuring pats, friendly talk, and little jokes. He listened attentively to every complaint and to all recitals of pain, discomfort, and trouble, and cheerfully soothed, or promised relief. His bedside manner was so personal, so warm and pleasant, that his very presence seemed a promise of quick good health.

The other intern was short, heavy, graceless, and taciturn. If he had any questions to ask, they were brief. His usual answer was some kind of muffled grunt. Most of the time he listened impassively to anyone who had the nerve to mention complaints, and seemed not to hear. When he was through with one patient, he moved on to the next in the same morose, silent fashion.

As you would expect, the first intern was a very popular man. But not the second. In fact, he was complained about to relatives, nurses, and staff doctors.

I happened to be in a position to see what the patients couldn't see—what happened when the two doctors left the ward.

The popular man did all that was expected of him. He made notes on charts, ordered medications and treatment, and left a number of helpful errands for others to run. He did everything he had to do. Then the problem, out of sight, was out of mind.

The second intern also wrote up his charts, but that was just the beginning of his work. He remembered every complaint, every known fact, every symptom and diagnostic sign of every patient, and took nothing for granted. He studied far into the night, consulted more experienced doctors, and pondered the full range of possible laboratory tests. He never cared whether the patients knew how hard he worked in their behalf. All that concerned him was to restore them to health. That was thanks enough.

This second intern is now my doctor, and yours. He has lost the shyness he once tried to conceal behind his grim expression, and his patients love him. He has not lost his habit of hard work, and can still, nine years later, remember the patients he treated as an intern, and their illnesses and treatments.

I am not tall, or handsome, or cheerful, but in our family I am the first intern, and your mother is the second. I am the friend who suffers the fewest inconveniences on your behalf, yet receives the most thanks. Your mother is the friend who sacrifices most, who labors hard and unseen, and whose thanks is, more often than not, a complaint.

I have given up very little in life to be your father and your friend. I support you, but I make my living doing the work of my choice. My labors bring me reward, thanks, and recognition. I have not had to give up my name, my identity, and my occupational freedom.

I do very little for you that is inconvenient, irksome, routine, or unpleasant, yet I always seem to be the source of favors and pleasures. Whenever you get an extra dollar, or use of the car, or join me in hunting, or exchange man-to-man confidences, these friendly benefits seem to come from me alone, and make me seem a pretty good guy. Neither of us, I am ashamed to say, appreciates the fact that our close, friendly times together are often made possible by the lonely labors and unthanked consent of your mother, and that our friendship is her gift.

The money I earn and give you is equally earned and given by her, but I am the one who is thanked for being generous. And I can't count how many of our father-son hours together as companions were paid for by her, how many routine and drab chores she freed us from without a word so that we might be friends.

I have given you much of many things, but I

have given you little of the greatest gift of all. You see this gift in many disguises when you see it at all—as good meals, ironed shirts, errands run, room cleaned, personal favors done. All the routine chores performed in your behalf represent time, and time is another word for the hours and minutes of her allotted time on earth. This is the quiet, willing gift she makes, and which I give seldom; the time that has to be deducted from the leisure hours of one person's life to enrich the hours of another's.

Like most cared-for children, you probably take your mother's way of life as "natural," or view it as her job, with no thanks or recognition needed from you. But abandoned and neglected children will tell you very readily that a mother's care is not something to take for granted. Although it is every child's birthright, it is by no means guaranteed. The world is full of people who have never known their rights.

Perhaps you feel that your mother works hard in your behalf merely because she loves you. But love isn't a good enough answer. There are mothers who love their children with all their hearts but who would not wash a dirty shirt if it might endanger the loveliness of their hands. There are mothers who dote on their children and raise them on peanut-butter-and-jelly sandwiches because they hate the work of cooking. There are mothers who would die for their children, but who would not cut down on their social engagements or abandon any of their own pleasures for their children's sake.

It is not natural force or love that provides you with a mother who works for your welfare without recognition, with few thanks, often at the expense of her own dreams and desires. Love alone could not sustain her as she prods you along the paths of righteousness regardless of your howls, your rudeness and you apparent disregard of her opinions and ideals. This, my boy, takes a true friend. A better friend than I or anyone else can ever be.

What it takes, I suppose, is a capacity for anonymity that most men simply don't have. It is this capacity that enables a woman to accept a role in life that demands the sacrifice of her name, the dedication of her person, and the sublimation of her own needs and wants to the needs and wants of others. She must do this knowing that those to whom she trades full hours in exchange for empty ones appreciate her sacrifices the least. And, just like a character in mythology who has been cast in a spell, she knows that to cry out to husband and children for the recognition and appreciation she deserves is to lose all chance of it forever. Few men, I repeat, could face life on these terms, yet most women do. And that, among other reasons, is why your mother, not your father, is the best friend you have.

I would like to close this letter with a few words about the woman you call mother.

The woman you call mother, and who has always been twenty-five years older than you, was very near your present age when I first met her and fell in love with her. And this woman who, in your mind, has never been conceded youth, has never in my mind grown older than the day we met.

There is a small miracle that takes place in our house when you and your sister are gone and your mother and I are alone. Once out of your sight, once freed from the roles we play for you, we emerge in private as the same two youngsters who met in the rain on a college campus.

She is and always will be the slender girl in blue jeans who was the liveliest and ablest member of the college theater-stagehand crew. I am and always will be the 120-pound boy who went to dinner at her college dormitory wearing my 150-pound brother's new suit so that I would look as nice as possible.

I wish you could join us when we are like that, somehow freed of the experience that automatically returns us to middle age the moment we appear in your eyes. Then I think you would understand, without benefit of language, what I am trying to spell out for you now—with questionable success.

It is the older woman you have lived with since birth who is your mother. It is this girl, almost your own age, this impossible combination of youth and experience, your mother's *self* as she always was and will be, who is your friend.

WHY I
AM NOT
YOUR PAL

I AM
writing this letter to explain why I have de-
liberately broken the first promise I ever made to
you.

The promise was made when you were about a
week old, on the day we brought you home from

the hospital. As I got my first really good look at you, when you were finally in our house as a member of the family, I promised you—and myself—that I would be more than just a father to you. I promised that you and I would be real pals.

Now, sixteen years later, we both know that I have not kept that vow. I am not your pal.

A great deal has been and is being written about the need for parents and children to be buddies. We are told it is not enough to give a child a home, understanding, material advantages, education, guidance, discipline, and love; that nothing can take the place of companionship.

This is a noble sentiment, but the attempt to live it to the letter has produced floods of childish tears (many of them yours), thunders of manly oaths (many of them mine), and ruined many a genuine relationship between parent and child.

You and I are, at this time, closer friends than are some fathers and sons, and not as close as others. (There may even be some who actually are pals.) I hope, with each day that you grow away from me as my child, you will grow closer to me as a friend. But even when you are a grown man, with a home and family of your own, I doubt that we can be buddies. If as adult men we like each other, we can be closer friends and companions than is now possible. But even then, although I will love you as much as ever, my buddies will be other old men, and yours will be other young husbands, just as now my real buddies are grown men, and yours are other boys.

I am not your pal because I have discovered, after much trial and error, that I don't want to be your pal, and you really don't want to be mine. I am not willing to give up the one relationship with you that is mine alone. It is worth too much to be exchanged for mere equality with your pals for the moment. Likewise, I think you would object if I tried to become your buddy at the expense of being your father. And this would be the cost of the trade.

Who and what are pals? Your pals are those friends of whom you most approve *as they are,* and who in turn most approve of you *as you are.* You are drawn together because you have more in common than with your other acquaintances. Yours is a voluntary association that is held together only by mutual approval. When, as so often happens, the approval ceases to be mutual or you are physically separated, the palship dissolves.

You will have many different pals as you move through high school, college, and into adult life. And in each new time and place, new buddies will provide you with the same kind of satisfactions your old ones did. Palship will continue to be based on the maximum amount of mutual, uncritical approval, and the minimum amount of mental, emotional, physical, and ethical conflict. It will also be based on proximity. These are the rules for being pals, and they apply to my pals and your mother's as well as to yours.

Being father and child, you and I are not off to a very good start toward being buddies. Our relationship is not voluntary, temporary, or equal, nor is it supported by so fragile a base as mutual, uncritical approval.

As your father, my strongest instinct and first duty is to advise, coach, guide, and control you. When we are in public together, others expect me to assume and exercise control over you. When you are out of my sight, the community expects me to function as your boss—even by remote control. And, most important of all, you yourself expect your mother and me to be your parents above anything else we are to you.

You depend on your pals for approval, but your parents are the only two people in the world upon whom you can safely depend for *disapproval*. We are the only ones you can trust implicitly to advise, guide, criticize, and control you whether it hurts you or ourselves, whether you like it or not, even if it means temporary loss of your friendship and good will.

I suppose you depend on us the way a pilot depends on his radio beam, confident it will start to beep the moment he swerves off course. You may be a stubborn and wilful pilot at times and insist on your right to fly by visual contact instead of by instrument, but you still depend on the beeps to sound when they are supposed to. If they didn't, you would lose faith in the accuracy, sensitivity, and reliability of the instrument itself. You would have nothing to trust your life to when the fog closed in.

Although you will have new pals all through life, you will always have the same two parents; no one else can ever completely take our place or exactly match our feelings for and our relationship with you.

We are physically, legally, and emotionally responsible for your life, and glad of it. Your welfare, behavior, personality, thoughts, and growth will always be our primary concern. Always, before we are anything else to you, we are your father and mother. Ours is the only relationship you will know that can thrive and develop and deepen through disagreement. It is the only relationship that may actually be strengthened by conflict, that is not corroded by time or faded by distance. Perhaps the difference between your pals and your parents is that your pals are people who like you now for the kind of person you seem to be; your parents will love you forever, regardless of what else you are, because you are their son.

Although I am neither pal nor buddy, I am your good and devoted friend. Forcing myself on you as a playmate—or having you forced on me— is no substitute for the friendly, if limited, associations we can and do enjoy. Your friendship with me and mine with you do not depend on how many activities we try to share as equals, but in our ability to recognize those areas in which we can—or cannot—happily share each other's company as father and son.

Because I have no illusions about being or becoming your buddy, we have both been spared pain. I never resented and you have never felt guilty about the fact that when you were little and I used to take you to the high-school football games, you would desert me the moment we were inside the stadium to run off with your classmates. That was as it should be. Similarly, it bothered neither you nor me that a few years later you obviously preferred the company of your contemporaries to mine. When I was gathering material for a book on automobile dirt-track racing, I used to take you along to the track. Neither of us suffered from the fact that as soon as we reached the pits, you always rushed off to meet the drivers' sons, who had become your buddies.

Similarly, more recently, you have spent a great deal of time in our garage trying to get an ancient automobile back into running condition. You have consulted me about your rebuilding problems, but you have not invited me to join the work —possibly because I am an indifferent mechanic but more likely because it is more fun to work with buddies than with fathers.

I am all for our companionship whenever and wherever and however we can share it naturally and without strain, but there is something to be said for the seemingly remote role I often fill as father-friend. As such, my special function is sometimes to provide the dollar, or the transportation, or the tool, or the shotgun shells, that make it possible for you to meet with and enjoy the companionship of your buddies. As such, it is also my friendly but fatherly function sometimes to deny you these pleasures. I think you understand my position as father-friend; you have even let me know as much.

Some time ago, on a stormy, subzero night, you asked for a ride across town, where you had a date with some friends. I remember growling as we stepped out into the swirling snow and biting cold, "Boy, it takes a real pal to turn out on a night like this. . . ." And I remember your turning to me with a grin and saying, "Or a Dad."

More than once, when you and your buddies were in our garage with the radio going full blast, I have stopped in for a look at the work. And

more than once, in this secure home shelter, working with your own tools and your own pals, I have
received from you a look of affection, friendship,
love, and appreciation that no mere pal or buddy
of yours will ever receive.

WILL YOU
LIVE HAPPILY
EVER AFTER?

T HERE
is no better reason to marry than being romantically in love. And yet—as you must be aware by
now—it is sadly true that many romantic matches
never go the route; that some of the happiest court-
ships end up as the most unhappy marriages.

When the time comes that you want to get married, I am sure it will be to a girl you love deeply and romantically, and who feels the same way about you. Between you, you will share everything that makes two young people want to be married. But will you (I wonder now, and will be wondering on your wedding day) share enough of what makes people want to *stay* married?

No matter what you two know, feel and believe about each other when you walk to the altar, neither of you will know what kind of mate you are marrying until you live together as husband and wife. The future of your marriage will depend not only on what you each feel toward and expect from the other, but what you both feel toward and expect from marriage itself.

My mother came to this country as a bride about sixty years ago. I remember her telling me that among the immigrants who packed the hold of the ship, there were some who really believed that the streets of America were paved with gold. All they would have to do to get rich, they thought, was to dig up baskets of golden paving stones.

When these people discovered their dreams

were false, some of them gave themselves up to disappointment and bitterness. Overlooking the real opportunities America offered, they blamed their misery not on their own childish expectations, but on the country they thought had "failed" them.

I am sure immigrants have become wiser since my mother's day, but I am not so sure about lovers. Every day thousands of romantic immigrants migrate to the fabled shores of matrimony —a paradise where, they have heard and truly believe, there are birds but no bugs, nuggets of bliss lie everywhere underfoot, and the fruits of happiness drop always in one's lap and never on one's head. When these migrants discover that achieving marital happiness involves work as well as wishes, they are likely to turn against marriage itself, and blame their misery on their partners, rather than on their own deluded dreams.

Too many young lovers come to marriage not as pioneers looking forward to building a new life, but as refugees seeking to escape the old. There are girls who marry to escape family discipline, and boys who marry to get away from schoolwork. People flee to matrimony from every kind of monster, real or imagined, that makes them dissatisfied with the life they've been leading. Somehow they expect the act of marriage to insulate them for all time from discipline, restraint, loneliness, routine or boredom with situation, place, job or self. This never-never land of no problems is to them the "happiness" that they seek.

Some of the blame for this fanciful idea of marriage must fall on cheap romantic movies, TV shows, books and stories which degrade love to the level of a crush—an emotional flare-up that is ignited by a cute haircut and extinguished by a facial blemish. The only real marital problem in these films and stories is finding the "right" person. Once this has been accomplished, all of life's other problems vanish forevermore. The wedding ring becomes a magic amulet that forever protects the happy young couple against every future hazard.

That, of course, is nonsense. There is nothing about marriage—even to the "right" person—that can protect you from poverty, illness, disappointment or despair; nothing about being married that automatically guarantees tranquillity or ecstasy.

Does this mean that in real life marriage is inferior to marriage in second-rate fiction? Not at all. It is infinitely superior!

What triumphs in escape stories is not love, but a kind of empty pseudohappiness which is dependent on the absence of problems. What results is not a bond between living men and women in a living world, but an alliance of robots who kiss.

Whatever is idle falls into decay. Unused machines rust, untilled soil becomes choked with weeds, unneeded people lose the will to live. The magic of marriage is that it creates meaningful goals to work for, struggle for, sacrifice for. It is the joint struggle that gives the relationship its meaning, and keeps people alive.

If you will notice, the next time you see a cheap movie or read a pulp romance, the problems and joys of life are separated like the "good guys" and the "bad guys" in a Western story. When the hero and the heroine marry at last, the bad-guy-problems vanish, and only the good-guy-joys remain.

In real life it is often impossible to distinguish between problems and joys because they are so often one and the same. In the marriage between your mother and myself, you and your sister are without doubt our greatest source of joy. At the same time, you are the source of our deepest worries, concerns, difficulties and heartaches. Yet, without the problem of children there could be no joy of children.

This is true for every other challenge of married life. Meeting and solving problems is not a burden, but a labor of love, whether they be problems of personal adjustment, family living or earning bread. Meeting problems together is the way that honeymooners grow into life partners. The greatest problem your mother and I will face in our marriage will come when you and your sister are grown and gone, and we have nothing to live for but our own peace and pleasure. If our happiness is to survive, we will have to find another meaningful struggle in which to enlist our marriage.

I hope I have not given the impression that I think romantic love is without strength or substance. Romantic love is the foundation upon which a good marriage must be built and forever stand. It is a foundation that supports not only the problems of life, but also the many forms of love that grow out of being married.

There are some who sneer at it as a form of sensual desire that will vanish as soon as the novelty of being married has worn off. This is not true. Real love begins only after novelty has worn off. Only then can you begin to love not merely to gain pleasure, but to give it.

I will go further and say that you cannot really love a woman romantically until she has been your wife. Before marriage, the most you can love her for is what you hope she will mean to you after you are married. After marriage, you are able to love her also for what she has been and is to you.

If romantic love seems less obvious in marriage than in courtship, it is because romantic love is the only kind of love that sweethearts know. In marriage, it takes its place as one of many loves that is produced by living, working and meeting problems together.

You are familiar with the expression that "love conquers all," and it is true more times than it is false. But love cannot conquer that which it evades, avoids or flees; only that against which it contends with courage and dignity.

Marriage is not only an action to achieve love, but an act of faith. The girl you marry is the one you are willing to trust with your life and the lives of your children. The wedding is not an end to being single, but a beginning of being married.

Real marriage offers every romantic satisfaction and emotional protection promised by the happy-ever-after story, but in real life the search and struggle for happiness begins, not ends, when the girl is won. A real marriage between real people in a real world is not a refuge for the fearful, but a port of embarkation for the brave. The many true loves of marriage are not fading remnants left over from the courtship, but new fabrics whose designs must be jointly drawn to decorate, and whose yarns must be jointly woven to protect.

You will discover (if you earn the right) that the many true loves of marriage are created by its joys and heartaches, its labors, its worries, its sacrifices and failures, its triumphs of joint endeavor and understanding. You will discover that it is not the ride into the sunset, but the everyday struggles for bread and roof, and against dirty necks and dust that add up, in this life, to the most common, ordinary, universal, wonderful love story ever told.

THE WHYS
AND WHEREFORES
OF FAMILY FIGHTS

ON THE
day that you and some girl in your future decide
to become engaged, you will probably promise
each other that, unlike other married couples, you
two will never quarrel.

I hope you never keep this promise.

I admit that family conflicts are unpleasant, but they are often essential to family cohesion, and necessary for the happiness of its members. I say this to head off a question my previous letters may have raised in your mind: If marriage and family are the source of all the joys and satisfactions I have claimed them to be, why isn't family life always harmonious? Why, instead, is there so often open conflict?

I use the word conflict—a polite way of saying that, since the first time I picked you up with trembling hands, held you to my heart and wept with joy and awe and sadness, I have nagged, scolded, insulted, quarreled and contended with you. And, since first you nestled trustfully and safely in my arms, you have flouted, mocked, insulted, yelled, sworn and swung at me.

CONFLICT IS A FACT OF LIFE

I use the word conflict—a polite way of saying that, ever since your mother and I promised to love and cherish each other forever, we have had every kind of row, for every kind of real or imagined reason—complete with raised voices, flushed faces, slammed doors and cutting remarks about each other's characters and intelligence.

And yet, to answer the question I have put in your mouth, I believe that when it comes to important issues, our family life *is* harmonious.

The fact that we often fight does not mean we aren't getting along. The absence of open family conflict does not in itself mean happiness, any more than the absence of shooting between two countries means peace. Sometimes it means only that one of the parties isn't ready to fight—yet.

In any relationship as intimate and intricate as marriage, there are bound to be many causes for conflict, many sources of annoyances and disagreements. I suppose life would seem more pleasant if these differences could be worked out in quiet, good fellowship, but that's not always possible. Nor am I sure that it's always a worthwhile goal.

LETTING FEELINGS OUT

What we're talking about now is not a panel discussion of behavior problems or a polite exchange of opinions. Family rows are contests not only of beliefs, but of feelings. The jealousies, angers, frustrations and injustices of daily life involve deep emotions, and engender emotional battles. To what extent, when angry passions are aroused, should they be suppressed to avoid an open quarrel?

I'm sure you don't need to be told that, on the whole, I'm for letting feelings come out. Actually, I would be more disturbed if you and I weren't in conflict than I am because we are. If there were no contest, it would mean that one of us had given up the natural fight of his generation and family position. You are too old to accept my definition of life without argument, just as you are too young for me to accept yours.

Although ours is essentially a training battle, it is also a real struggle to retain power on my part, and for independence on yours. And, in our fights, I must rule according to my nature, and you rebel according to yours. We both have tempers that ignite at a spark, but which subside as quickly. Our explosions are violent, but they clear the air. Afterward there are no smoldering resentments to foul the atmosphere.

I have heard some parents boast that their children so respect (or fear) their authority that the children wouldn't dare talk back, be impudent or openly defiant. I may be wrong, but I would rather, when you are angry with me that you shake your fist at my offending face, than have you slink outside and shake it helplessly at the sky. After all, if you can't fight openly and honestly for your own integrity against a father who loves you, how will you ever be able to fight for it against the world?

It is no accident that we become the closest of friends after the worst of arguments. Conflict does more than release tension. It is a reassurance that you can continue to be yourself in your own home without penalty. Because you feel secure enough in my love to direct your hostilities and angers toward me, you also trust me enough to confide your hopes and longings.

This is also true in the relationship between husband and wife. I have met couples who boasted that in ten, fifteen or twenty years of marriage, they never had a quarrel. This sounds to me more like a dirge than a symphony. It indicates a lack of passionate feeling that, in marriage, is almost indecent.

Of course there may be people who are so spiritless they never have reason to clash. Or, if they have, choke off their feelings in the interest of harmony. I do not envy such people. If there is to be real feeling in a relationship, there must be no barriers beyond which emotions are forbidden to range. You can't limit the heat of marital conflict without, at the same time, cooling the heat of marital love.

I do not know, when you marry, to what extent you and your wife will need to express yourselves in quarrels or argument. Whatever that need is, I hope you will have the courage to satisfy it. I hope your marriage will not be so fragile that you must keep silent for fear of swamping it with a wrong word or sinking it with a wrong look.

Conflicts between husband and wife are not foreign irritants that blow into your life on a chance wind. They are created by marriage from the raw materials that are you, she, your demands on each other, and by the very loving, sharing and closeness of your lives. And these conflicts, whether they be trivial or serious, will cause you real trouble only if you attempt to deny them their right to exist.

The unhappiest husbands or wives I ever knew were those whose mates had denied them the right to argue or quarrel, or "have it out" when a fight was indicated and needed. Of all frustrations in life, this may well be one of the worst.

The frustrated and silenced boy is likely to take out his anger behind the wheel of his car; the frustrated husband to drown his rage in drink; the frustrated wife to strike back by wasting her husband's money. In the interest of safety, sobriety and solvency, it is better for the family to argue together all night than to have family "peace" at the price of private rage.

When you marry, you will want to do everything in your power to make your wife happy. Remember, you will be marrying a real human being with a full set of emotions. Don't, by exchanging promises never to quarrel, marry half the girl you fell in love with, or give her half yourself as husband.

If promises are called for, promise her the right to differ with you whenever and however she wants or needs, and ask the same right for yourself. For with this joint guarantee that you can always be and fight for your honest selves without jeopardy, you guarantee each other emotional freedom in which love is rooted, and marriage thrives.

WHEN DOES
A BOY
BECOME
A MAN?

L̲AST
Saturday you and I disagreed on how late you
should be allowed to stay out. When I refused to
extend your curfew, you complained that I was
not treating you like an adult. This has become
your standard answer whenever you can't have

your own way. But what you really mean is that I don't go along with your idea of what constitutes adulthood.

Let me put it this way: I do not pretend you are a grown man because you are a 16-year-old boy. I am not as you are deceived by a few similarities of plumage, diet and song into identifying you as a genuine adult. You may be as big and strong and capable as many adults (and you probably argue better than most!), but only a child would maintain—and sincerely believe—that his manhood can be measured by the lateness of the hour his father permits him to stay out at night.

Recently I attended an assembly of teen-agers that was addressed by a grown man. He seemed to believe that the way to get the audience on his side was to pretend that he was one of them. He jittered and jiggled, made odd faces, spoke disdainfully about adults, and labored to use a great deal of what he thought was current teen-age slang.

Later, I heard the kids talk with amusement and contempt about his efforts to appear as one of them by imitating what he thought was teen-age behavior. It was obvious from their comments that the speaker would have commanded more respect and attention if he had appeared as a grown man and not as a caricature of a boy. All he did was make more obvious the gulf of years that lay between him and his audience.

The kids could see how silly it was for an adult to pretend he was a boy, but they could not see the same thing in reverse. After the assembly I saw teen-age boys swaggering down the street with forbidden cigarettes in their mouths, manfully cursing as they swaggered. Others roared away in their cars, belligerently demonstrating their "right" to the streets. I saw little teen-age girls teetering along on spike heels in tight dresses, with extravagantly styled and dyed hair. All this, I am sure, because they believed they could impress the world with their maturity if they imitated behavior that, to them, appeared to be adult.

All this reminded me of a fable I used to read aloud when you were little, about the donkey who longed to be a lion. The donkey, if you recall, covered himself with a lion's skin, crept in among the lions, and lay down quietly among them. When the lions took no notice of him, and seemingly accepted him as one of them, the donkey was filled with joy and confidence. It seemed to him that he had actually become a lion, and he thought of donkeys with contempt. All went well until evening, when the lions began their customary evening roaring. The little donkey, completely fooled by his own disguise, lifted his head and roared with them. What came out, of course, was a donkey's bray. Whereupon the lions fell upon him and devoured him.

The moral applies equally to boys and men. Human victims of self-deception are likely to be devoured by the lions of reality.

If the extremes of behavior among teen-agers represented nothing more than a little natural daydreaming and imitation, they could be overlooked. But the danger in them—as in your attitude toward how late you stay out—is that they look like real lion skins, and are so employed.

I can understand why you and your friends are eager to become adults, and to enjoy the freedoms, privileges and even the bad habits that are denied to you as children. What you fail to see is that these freedoms and privileges are routine and minor by-products of being an adult. They are not, as many of you believe, the components of genuine maturity.

Look around a typical American town. Ninety percent of the people who could stay up all night are in bed by ten. Ninety percent of the people who have the legal right to smoke wish they were able to give up the habit. Ninety percent of the people who have the right to buy and drink all the liquor they want are sober. Ninety percent of the grown single men and women, who have the opportunity to be as sexually casual as they wish, are looking for a mate with whom to settle down. What it all adds up to is the fact that the huge majority of men and women are mature. And yet children seem to believe that the way to prove themselves adult is to imitate the unstable, destructive, irresponsible minority.

It is possible for children to convince themselves and each other that disobedience, late hours, smoking, drinking, sexual experiments and the rest actually transform them into adults. When this happens they often begin to despise their own contemporaries and the tasks that are appropriate to their age. They often come to resent not only parental direction and control, but to resist and resent school, and avoid normal teenage activities and patterns. The boy who believes that a deep voice and bad habits have made him manly wants to quit school, get a job, buy a car and "be a real man." The girl who has talked and acted and dressed her way out of being her age believes that getting married at once will result in her being an instant woman.

Several days ago, our newspaper interviewed a group of teen-agers on what they thought it meant to be adult. Some of the boys seemed to envision maturity as a time when they would be big enough to be irresponsible without having to account to anyone for their behavior. One girl of seventeen wanted to get married right away so she could escape her parents, be an adult and be in a position where "nobody can tell me what to do."

I felt sorry for these boys whose goal in life was to be failures as men. I felt sorry for the girl who didn't seem to understand that the absence of orders did not mean the absence of duties; that the reason no one seems to tell adults what to do is that they do what has to be done without being told.

It is a sad thing when children renounce their own generation and try to sneak into maturity as though it were a border to be crossed under cover of darkness. They do not become free and equal citizens of the adult world. They become half-formed semi-adults who are as out of place in the adult world as they thought they were in the child's. They are the young, untrained, unedu-cated, unprepared and inept people who have trouble finding and keeping the worst jobs, whose hasty escape-marriages fall apart at the first tremor, whose babies often become public charges. They try to flee the restraints of being adults as once they fled the restraints of being children. Only now there is nowhere to run. They are the don-keys who are so taken in by their lion costumes that they attempt to roar and are devoured when, in fact, they bray.

You complain that I do not treat you like an adult. My reply is, I would rather treat you like what you are. And at sixteen, you are a boy and you belong in a boy's world, accepting a boy's responsibilities, dreaming a boy's dreams, learning a boy's freedoms, appreciating your boyish years. Being a successful boy is the best guarantee in the world that you will be a successful man.

In a few years, time and experience will make

you an adult. When it does, I will treat you like an adult. It will be impossible for me to do otherwise. I don't know when that time will come, or when you will discover that it has. But I can give you one clue. When the time comes that you no longer feel the necessity to prove to me, to your friends, to the world or to yourself that you are a man—you will have become one.

WHY I
(DON'T)
UNDERSTAND
YOU

ALMOST every day I get letters from young readers who compliment me on my ability to understand teen-agers. And, almost every day, you complain that the trouble with me as a father is, I don't understand you.

LETTERS TO A TEEN-AGE SON   80

I hope my readers are right. I know you are. For I think I do understand you somewhat as a teen-ager, and I certainly don't understand *you*.

It is important to your welfare and happiness that both of us understand you as an average, Middle Western, suburban teen-age boy. That's the whole point of my work here. But when it comes to understanding the inner, private, special, lifetime *you*—that is *your own* inner, private, special, lifetime task. Your happiness as a human being depends not on how well others seem to understand you, but on how soon and how successfully you discover and understand yourself.

At first thought your complaint of being misunderstood seems a simple problem, the answer to which is more understanding on my part.

Only, that isn't the problem at all.

The most difficult lifelong problem any of us has, is learning to tell the difference between *being* misunderstood, *feeling* misunderstood *and not being able to understand.*

Very often, the hollow teen-age complaint that "My parents don't understand me" can be translated into its real meaning, which is, "My parents won't let me have my own way."

Later on in life, this same tune is sung to the words of "My wife doesn't understand me," "My boss doesn't understand me" or (very popular around age twenty) "The world doesn't understand me." And most of the time, the correct translation begins with the words "*I* don't understand . . ."

In all instances the problem is not one of understanding, but of negotiation. The cry represents an inability to see any point of view other than one's own, plus an unwillingness to look.

I have heard boys and girls complain they were misunderstood at home because their parents wouldn't let them stay out all night, go off on mixed, unchaperoned weekends, drive a car without a license, quit school to get married or take a laboring job to support a car, or wouldn't buy them a car, give them all the money they wanted or allow them to smoke or drink.

The reason parents don't allow these things isn't because they don't understand how teenagers feel, or have forgotten what it is like to be young, but because they do understand, and have not forgotten.

What we are up against here is that the child

demands to be "understood" as the person he is at the moment, and the parents' job is to understand him as he is, as he was and as he is going to be. Since the most difficult thing in the world for a child is to see himself ever being or feeling different than he does at the moment, he feels misunderstood. And *feeling,* but not really *being* misunderstood, is a convenient tent for a teenager to sulk in, and avoid the truth that would reveal to him his own immaturity—his inability to understand.

If, through some miracle tonight, I could arise in the morning as the most perfect, understanding father in the world, you would continue to feel misunderstood unless there was another miracle, in your room, that enabled you to understand when you were being understood.

The way it is, and was and always will be, there is that private self of yours that no one will ever understand completely, no matter how hard you try to explain yourself. And there is the just-another-human-being you, that is as old as the human race, and so obvious and common that even strangers can identify and understand you at a glance.

That is what I meant when I said I understood you as a teen-ager, but I didn't understand *you*.

For example, I know why you are anxious to own and drive your car. I don't know why you prefer tinkering with a car to playing football.

I know why you are impatient to be a grown man. I don't know what your definition of maturity is.

I know a great many of your opinions. I know hardly any of your thoughts.

I know why you want to stay out late at night with your friends. I don't know what it takes to be your friend.

I know why you are restless in school. I don't know why you like to read and have no head for math.

I know what you want at the moment. I don't know what you long for.

I know why you wear the kind of clothes you do, the way you do. I don't know why you like blue and dislike green.

I know you fall in love. I don't know what there is about a girl that causes you to love her.

I know what kind of boy you seem among other boys. I don't know you.

I understand you. I don't understand *you*.

You know, it is important that I understand you, and it is important that you feel understood, but there is another need that might be just as important. And that is your need, while calling for more understanding, to be misunderstood.

There are times when it is necessary for a teenager to feel misunderstood, particularly by his parents. At these times the only thing that infuriates him more than trying to understand him is to prove that you do. Because that makes him go to a lot of trouble to prove that you don't. And one of the most delicate operations of parenthood is to guess correctly the times and ways in which the teen-ager needs to feel misunderstood.

There is, in all of us, a need to feel that we are complex, unique people, and that the emotions we feel are not only new to us, but new emotions. And these highly personal, private emotions and feelings are ruined for us if some other person bleats, "I know just exactly how you feel. I felt just like you when I was your age."

We parents say this with the best of intentions. We say it to relieve tensions, to dispel anxieties and loneliness, to reassure, to show that certain strange and troubling emotions and actions are normal and universal, and to make the child's way through life a little smoother, a little more intelligible, a little more pleasant.

But in trying to be too helpful, too understanding, too kind, too close, too perceptive, too smart and too discerning, we destroy some of life's needed mystery, and diminish the fearful joy of growth.

It is as though an explorer were to imagine himself first on some wild and undiscovered land, then find that not only has someone else been there before him, but that someone else has already pacified the savages, built roads through the jungles, classified the flora and fauna, made the drinking water safe and turned one's dangerous, exciting adventure into a dreary guided tour, and a color slide show of what it "used to be like."

I know when my parents correctly interpreted some obscure mood or troubled action of mine, I often felt cheated rather than assisted. It made me feel that instead of living my own, new, special life, I was merely living theirs over again.

I know I baffled my parents when I rejected their interest in my welfare, and angrily spurned their kindly attempts at advice. But sometimes it is an awful thing to be told on Monday how you are going to feel on Tuesday—then feel that way. It is deadly to hear a parent's voice telling you accurately how you feel about girls, what your thoughts are about finding a place in the world, about your doubts, your dreams, your *day*dreams and even, all too exactly, the nature of your regret at having acted foolishly. Sometimes, when you feel that every step you take is in a parental foot-step, you don't even want to walk.

The reason I disobeyed my parents and did foolish things against their advice wasn't because I thought they were wrong about life. It was be-cause I knew, deep down, that they were right. And it was more necessary for me to create my own darkness to stumble around in, than to be led around disaster by their light. And how awful when they made the mistake of letting me know that they *understood*.

I loved my parents, but they were just ordinary people. And it devastated me to think that I was so obvious, so lacking in individuality and com-plexity, that these ordinary people could troll in my darkest depths with a bent pin, and always come up with a fish.

In some ways, I think it was because my parents were so understanding and knowledgeable that I left home for good when I was sixteen years old. Only among strangers did I feel comfortably inscrutable and unpredictable. I was able to relax only when those who looked into my eyes were unable (I thought) to see a framed portrait of my soul.

I was wrong, of course. That part of me that was myself was never known to my parents, any more than it is known now by my wife, children, friends or even myself. But that part of me that was teen-age, and universal and just plain young human being, was as obvious to my stranger-teachers at the State University of Iowa as it had been to my parents in New York. Not being able to separate my two selves, I went around feeling mysterious, unfathomable and inscrutable, unaware that most of my feelings and "discoveries" were older than the campus, and that most of the other students were thinking and feeling the same way. The reason I felt so comfortably enigmatic and misunderstood was that no one bothered to tell me that I was understood. I thought I was fitting college life to my needs. I never knew that college life had been planned, created and organized to fit mine. The secret of its success was that it never told me so, in so many words.

We feel odd, strange, interesting, frightening, joyful, wonderful and terrible emotions when we are teen-agers, and we would rather not be told that someone else is more aware of the turmoil inside us than we are. There is much to discover about the world and ourselves when we are young, and we don't want someone else cheating us of the chance to plant our own flag on new soil, and claiming the area for our own sovereign.

We want what amounts to an equal opportunity to be young, foolish, experimental, wrong, tortured, amazed and overwhelmed; an equal opportunity to learn the bitter from the sweet by tasting, and not being told. Above all, we need to preserve the feeling that, for all our outward resemblance to others, we are special, indecipherable, unique and incomprehensible. We need the security of closed doors between our inner selves and the outer world.

Too much help, too much good advice, too much demonstrated loving understanding, too much guidance, can make us feel emotionally naked and unprotected, and make our lives seem shallow and secondhand. Sometimes the kind of understanding we need most is all the blank "misunderstanding" we can get.

DOWN WITH DISAPPOINTMENT!

I HAVE been thinking about the various wrongs I have done you over the years, all in the name of being your father. And I have concluded, with some surprise, that I have hurt you most at times I was trying to be kind.

There have been many times when, hoping to sound civilized, to be gentle in admonition and reassuring even in reproach, I have said to you, "I'm not angry with you, son, I'm just disappointed." How often, nobly intending to sustain your spirit, have I fed it these most poisonous of words!

There are defenses against direct and open attacks. One can meet anger with calmness, punishment with dignity, force with courage, accusations with rebuttals, criticisms with explanations. There is an opportunity to fight back, and to win. One's position has been attacked, but not one's identity.

My angers, irritations, annoyances and exasperations with you are *my* feelings, and touch you not internally. But my disappointment, voiced or expressed with a look, becomes *your* feeling. For to tell another you are disappointed in him is neither a blow he can ward off, nor a thrust he can parry. It is to plant in another's soul the seed of doubt, of failure, of unworthiness, of incompetence and of hopelessness.

I know this to be true. When I have sensed in you some deep and hidden feeling of disappointment in me, I have felt as in no other situation a helplessness for which there was no cry of help. It did not matter whether I felt you were right or wrong in your feeling. What mattered was, there was no argument, no fact, no logic, no smile or bribe or plea that could scale the sheer wall of your feeling. You had formed an emotional opinion, and there was nothing I could do about it but feel wronged and frustrated.

I have done the same thing to you. Thinking to appeal to your better self, and shame you into reform, I have denied you the rightful anger and punishment some specific action had earned. Instead, I kindly and coldly blamed you for not being, in the flesh, some ideal boy-image that existed in my own mind. How little I asked of you by being disappointed in you—merely that you be some dream of my own come true!

I think we fall into this trap of disappointment because we begin life as parent and child at the top, and for a while there seems no other direction to go but down.

When the child is small, and the real world ends at the front gate, his parents are the only adults in the world who are clear, necessary and worthwhile. They are, to the little child, the most wonderful, capable, strong, wise and sweet people on earth. From them all blessings flow.

But as the child grows, and the world expands, he begins to compare his parents with other adults. And it is a shock to discover that there are men who are richer, stronger, taller and wiser than Dad. And there are women who seem prettier, more gracious and more intelligent than Mom. Most painful of all is the discovery that other parents seem willing and able to provide their children with all the good things he would like to have.

How soon we become aware that our parents cannot (or will not) provide us with everything we want. That is, whatever it is we don't already possess. Do we have a gun? The lucky kid up the street has a bike. Do we have a bike? The lucky kid down the street has a gun. Do we have a bike and a gun? The luckier kid across the street has a newer bike and a more expensive gun. Do we have kind parents? The lucky kid over there has rich ones. Do we have rich parents? The lucky kid has kind ones. Some lucky kids have brothers and sisters, and some lucky kids have none.

A few months ago I had to sit through a speech given by a loan company official before a group of teen-agers. He told his audience that as Americans, they had the right to possess the best of everything the world had to offer, the moment it became available. Not the right or the opportunity to earn, but the right to *have*.

The bankruptcy courts are filled with adults who have followed this self-indulgent philosophy to disaster, but it went over big with the kids. Why not? We are, as children, uncritically all-important to ourselves—which means all-important. And whether we get everything or not, we feel we naturally deserve the best—and if we lack anything, we are apt to feel that we have been cheated out of it.

Our own wants, desires and demands never seem unreasonable to us, and if our parents are unable to provide what we ask, we are more likely to accuse them of being inadequate than ourselves of being greedy.

As we reach adolescence it seems not that we grow larger, but that our parents shrink; not that we demand more, but that they provide less; not that we can see the world, but that they are blind

DOWN WITH DISAPPOINTMENT!   95

to it; not that we charge headlong into them, but that they are in our way; not that we learn, but that they become ignorant.

If our parents first disappoint us by not being able to provide everything we want, they add insult to injury when we become teen-agers by seeming to stand between us and everything we want to be.

The more we realize our parents are ordinary human beings, with many faults and limitations, the more likely we are to feel that they have failed us, and the more critical we become of them. Each day, with a kind of sad triumph, we discover new ways in which they are inferior first to other adults, and, finally, to ourselves.

In adolescence, the very time in life we are most critical of them, they become even more critical of us. Just as we resolve never to make their mistakes, they try to force us to repeat them. Just as we dread having any resemblance to them, they try to make us into carbon copies of themselves. Or so it seems.

Meanwhile, the parents are having their troubles. As the most perfect and loving of all little babies grows older and moves out of the house into the community, the parents begin to compare him with other children. (Or other parents do it for them.) And particularly if he is a first or only child, it is a shock to them to discover that there are other children his age who are (or seem) more capable, smarter, better-looking, better behaved, more dutiful and more mature than their own.

Comparisons may be odious, but they are inevitable, and can be beneficial. By learning to compare we learn to judge, and, presumably, to act more intelligently. At best, honest comparison enables parents to identify their child more accurately in his world, to recognize his strong and weak points, and to guide him accordingly.

I say at best, but parents are only human beings with children, and there is no law that says they have to be wise, good, sensitive, perceptive, expert and immune to error, if they were not so before.

Just as children are disappointed in their parents for not meeting some private specification for parenthood, so are there parents who are disappointed in their children for a similar reason.

Sadly, the world is filled with parents who are disappointed in their children because the children turned out to be themselves. There are fathers who reject their daughters because they were not born sons. There are fathers who evaluate their sons as human beings solely on the amount of interest and ability the boys show in sports, science, fighting, or whatever else the father is addicted to.

I have heard that in some suburban housing developments, offspring competition between mothers begins early and starts fast. The "human race" comes to mean that contest to see whose baby walks, talks, and is toilet-trained at the earliest age. And I have heard mothers, in public, with the child listening, describe him as something in the nature of a factory-second, because he spent an extra week in diapers.

These are extreme but not unusual cases. And we are all handicapped by similar emotional blinders.

It is an old parental habit to hold up other children as shining examples for our own. All we ask is that our dear child be as bright as Bill, as cheerful as Tom, as neat as Roger, as studious as Bernie, as courteous as Ralph, as helpful as Bob and so on. (For some reason we never see that he is more helpful than Bill, brighter than Bob, more cheerful than Roger, etc., etc.)

We think to do the child a favor when we cast around and find some other child for him to emulate. We hope, by giving him a living example of what one boy can accomplish, he will be encouraged to try the same thing for himself. What we forget from our own childhood days is that this kind of thing makes one feel his parents are disappointed because they have him for a child.

Right here I want to suggest a way to end forever that unfair, destructive phrase, "I'm (only) disappointed in you."

Let's never forget that the only time we have the right to be disappointed in others is when they fail to be what *they* claim, and not when they fail to be what we hoped.

May we never forget that, in themselves, the words "child" or "parent" or "father" or "son" are like the word "store."

We do not insist that, since all stores sell some things, any store we enter must sell anything or everything we want. We do not try to buy shoes from the butcher or meat from the cobbler, then walk out bitter and disillusioned because the "store" failed to meet our demands. We know enough to look for signs that say *shoe* store, or *meat* store, and order accordingly.

By the same token, we cannot insist that the words "child" or "parent" should automatically guarantee whatever level of relationship or performance that suits our fancy. Here too, before we can communicate intelligently, and with results, we must determine what kind of "store" we have for a child or a parent, making our demands in accordance with the kind of goods it carries, and the amount of stock on its shelves.

WELCOME ABOARD YOUR SHAKEDOWN CRUISE

Hᴏᴡ does it happen? How do we begin life as devoted parent and child, and, after years of living together, trying to love and please each other, end up as hostile strangers?

What happens along the way? Why can't we

get along nicely "any more"?

We grope for explanations like the survivors of a mysterious explosion, stunned as much by surprise as by the blast.

The answer is, I think, that we are getting along as normally and successfully as we ever did, and as nicely as is possible at this time in your life. There are good, honest reasons why havoc seems to break loose during adolescence.

What we call growing up would be understood better if we called it growing away, and growing toward. For it is the process of growing away from needing the care, protection, assistance, restraints, affection and companionship of your parents, and toward becoming your own, independent self.

This natural destiny of yours is not in dispute around this house. The whole purpose of my fathering is to enable you to get along without me.

If I am for you, why do I so often seem against you? If I want you to be independent, why do I try to rule you? If I want you to make your own decisions, why do I try to tell you what they should be? If I want you to make your own way in the world, why do I hold you back? Why is it, the closer you come to manhood, the more I seem to pick on you?

Let me put it this way:

When you were an infant, I probably was more anxious than you that you learn to stand alone. The moment you could stand alone, I was more fearful than you that you might fall. But once you could stand, you pushed my hand away if I tried to help you—yet you grabbed trustingly for my legs whenever you felt yourself toppling.

Later on I was pleased that you could walk and run, but appalled at the dangers into which your active legs carried you. You could see cars, but you were too young to comprehend traffic, or understand danger. I wanted you to run, yet I had to prohibit you from running into the street. Of course you were furious when I restrained you, and sometimes you ran into the street just to prove you could if *you* wanted to. But whenever you fell and hurt yourself, even while defying me, you wanted and expected me to come to your aid and comfort you. Later, you wanted to hold my hand when there was a street to cross, once you were able to understand the dangers of the street.

This urge to be independent of me when and how you choose, and to depend on me when and how you choose, is part of your natural process of outgrowing me. Our life has followed this same pattern from the simple problems of babyhood to the present complex physical and emotional problems of adolescence.

The way we stand now, I continue to rejoice at each new step you take toward maturity and independence, but I must also, over your protests, continue to steer you away from new dangers that you can often see, but cannot yet comprehend.

So there is nothing new about the basic nature of our oppositions and head-butting. What has changed has been the amount of conflict, the kind of issues involved and the way we feel about our encounters.

Our conflicts reach their peak when you become a teen-ager for the same reason that the white horses eat more than the black horses—there just happen to be more of them.

When you were a little boy our conflicts—if we can even call them that—were brief, isolated, infrequent little skirmishes having to do with the simple little problems of your babyhood. Days, perhaps weeks would pass without a really cross word between us. We had more good times together than we had bad, yet it would be wrong to say that we got along better than we do now. It was your small size that limited the number of ways and times in which it was possible for us to battle.

Now that you are a teen-ager, we seem to be in conflict much of the time, and over everything. Naturally! The fact that you are, for the first time in our lives, my physical, mental and emotional equal, enables us to meet on all fronts with all forces.

Now that you are a man in every way, except that you are still a boy, the freedoms you seek are a man's, even though your methods of achieving them are often those of a child.

Your need is not merely to stand alone, or walk across the street alone, but to think alone, plan alone, dream alone, experience alone, achieve alone, suffer alone and become your mature self alone.

Just as you once had to walk alone on trembling legs to prove that you were a little boy and not a baby, the time has come for you to prove—in

proving yourself a young man and not a boy—
that you can be intellectually and emotionally independent of me. But though you flee my advice
and brush away my affection, you still need me
close—*but hands off*—in case you begin to topple.

The fact that this growing-away process is natural does not mean, as we are likely to assume,
that it is easy. Nothing is more natural than reproduction, yet the time of birth, the actual period
of transition from fetus to baby, is a time of pain
and peril as well as joy. And hardly less violent
and hazardous, in its own way, is the "natural"
transition one makes from girl to woman, or from
boy to man.

It is what we are that creates the conflicts between us. It is who we are that decides how we
behave.

You know, when a new ship is built, it always
goes through a series of shakedown cruises before
it is assigned to active, equal duty with the fleet.
The ship is taken out to sea and run through every
possible beam-wracking and engine-cracking maneuver. Emergencies of every kind are simulated,
and every effort is made to discover, before the
ship is committed to action, all flaws in the con-

struction and handling of the ship, and in the ability of the commander and crew.

I suppose adolescence could be described as the time of our human shakedown cruises. A time when we shove off in an untried ship manned by a green crew to make short, violent practice runs in the safety of our home waters.

You are engaged in your final series of shakedown runs. This is your last chance to practice, without serious risk, being independent and grown-up. It is your last chance to claim, simultaneously, the privileges of an adult and the responsibilities of a child. It is your last chance to be a man in every way possible for a boy to be.

One of the things that makes us so miserable now is that our fights no longer seem to be waged over what you do, but over what you are. Although I say I criticize your actions, what I seem to dislike is you. When you buck my authority, what you seem to reject is me as your father.

This too is a phase of the normal shakedown cruise.

In your necessary effort to test your ship, you must simulate every emergency, including that of being an orphan. In order to prove your ability to stay afloat alone if you had to, you must prove you can survive now without the parental love, approval, direction and protection that has been essential to your survival until now.

This accounts for the different nature of our conflicts. No longer are you merely testing the extent of my authority as your father. What is under attack now is the relationship itself. The only way to practice getting along without parents is to pretend they don't exist. The only way to find out how to live without love and approval is to reject them, and fight them off.

This explains—in part—why it is sometimes impossible to please, satisfy or love you; why you are hostile in response to affection, disobedient to orders, scornful of concern and at odds with the family's way of life. It helps explain why you sometimes seclude yourself physically, mentally and emotionally from the family, yet cling to home.

It used to irritate me to see you reject my love, sneer at my ideals, scoff at my counsel, oppose my wishes—yet make all kinds of extravagant demands on me for service and purchases. I did not understand that the shakedown cruise often tests a few selected areas at a time.

When it was time for you to reject my love and friendship, it was also necessary to demand more money, more things, more favors, more "proof" that I loved you during the test. And I have noticed that when you want to stand on your own feet economically, and make very few "things" requests of me, you are your most affectionate and companionable with me.

This need to prove your seaworthiness by fighting with me and rejecting me is transient, but it is not a game. Unless the emotions are real, the test is worthless. Honest heartache and genuine tears are the price we pay for your ticket to manhood. But it is a small price compared to what we would have to pay for peace during adolescence— your future manhood itself.

ALL
ABOUT
DATING

I WANT
to tell you everything I think you *have* to know
about dating, and I believe it can be said in a few
hundred words.

Before you began to drive you were obsessed
by the automobile, and read everything about

cars you could get your hands on. You could re-
cite perfectly every maneuver necessary to start
and drive a car. You were convinced that you were
capable of getting behind the wheel without any
experience, and driving off at high speed.

When you began to drive you were confronted
by an element that has to be experienced to be
understood—motion. Your confidence and imagined skill melted into confusion when the added
factor of relentless *motion* forced situations and
sensations upon you that you could not even an-
ticipate until you experienced them. And faster
than you could cope with them.

This is also true of your relationship with girls,
and of "sex." Here too, there is an added factor
that makes a hash of mechanical information, ter-
minology and good intentions. And that is the
added factor of *emotion*.

Just as you become a good driver when you
experience and learn to control the fact of swift,
potentially dangerous motion, so you will be able
to survive romantically and sexually when you
learn to control and guide the forces of even
swifter, and in some ways more dangerous, emotion.

What can you do about it? You can remember this:

When you ask a girl for a date, you assume full responsibility for her welfare. From the time you take her from her home until you bring her home again, she is in your care. It is your duty to protect and preserve her from risk and harm, whether it be as her chauffeur, guide or suitor. She must be kept as safe from your affection of the moment as she is from the recklessness or unpleasantness of others. She must also be kept safe from her affection of the moment.

There is a negative, cold-blooded attitude among many boys that says, "It is up to the girl to draw the line"; that tries to get as much from a girl as one can, and claims it is her fault if matters go too far.

In a way it is up to the girl—if she happens to be out with an irresponsible, unprincipled or undisciplined boy. But believe me this: It is the boy who must assume complete responsibility for the girl if he would have any real claim to manhood. For it is this sense of responsibility that, *at any age,* really separates the men from the boys.

THE
REAL
YOU

AS AN
adolescent, your home, your family and your
school are the real world you live in at this moment. You don't have to like this world, or even
want to be a part of it. But unless you understand
this world, and your true place in it, you will not

live successfully with it—or with yourself.

We begin to understand ourselves only after we understand our environment, because only then do we make sense as individuals. It is your obvious duty to find out whether you live under water or in a tree *before* you decide whether you are a fish or a bird.

I have often heard some teen-ager say, "I eat and sleep at home, but I don't live there. I don't have anything to do with my parents, or have anything in common with them."

It is one thing for a teen-ager to *say* he eats and sleeps at home but doesn't *live* there, and quite another thing to be his parent.

When one must labor to provide his food, clothing, shelter and education, must clean up after his careless messes, iron his shirts, prepare his meals, care for him when he is sick, worry about him when he is late or unhappy; when one has to suffer his mannerisms and endure his tantrums, and teach him against his will the route to manhood; when his joys gladden one's heart, and his sorrows bring tears to one's eyes; when one is spurred by love of him to gladly arrange and subordinate one's own life to his best interests—he *lives* in that house with that family whether *he* knows it or not. And he has a great deal in common with his parents!

This feeling of aloofness and detachment from the home, and of not really belonging to it, is an illusion, often prompted by nothing more noble than physical laziness, or an unwillingness to face the facts of real life.

If you "refuse" to recognize the home-world and your place in it, you can without feeling guilty evade your responsibilities toward it.

If you "don't know" how much work you cause others, you can honestly pretend you don't cause any.

If you "don't know" your parents' limitations, you can ask everything of them with a clear conscience.

If you have "nothing in common" with your family, you can disassociate yourself from such unpleasant realities as their "inferior" social, racial or economic position—without feeling like a traitor to those who love you.

You can decide to be your own, individual, unaffiliated self, but you can't escape being one of us.

This isn't just a teen-age problem. No matter who we are, or how old we are, the two most difficult accomplishments in life are (1) to see ourselves as others see us, and (2) to be aware of the nature and amount of impact we have on the lives of others.

We have with us, at the time of this writing, something called "the beat generation." The title, as far as I know, is new, but the characters and speeches are as old as man's ability to feel sorry for himself.

The "beats" (whatever they are called when you are older; in my day it was the "lost" generation and the "lunatic fringe") are a living example of what happens when self-centered, overly introspective, ill-informed, daydreaming children grow older, but not more mature.

In the same way that children feel misunderstood in the home because they do not understand the home, the beats, failing to understand the world, take refuge in feeling misunderstood as a way of life.

If you examine beat literature and behavior,

you will find it exactly the substance and manner of the teen-agers I have mentioned.

Instead of saying, "My parents don't understand me," the beats say, "The world doesn't understand me." Instead of claiming to have nothing in common with their parents, the beats claim to have nothing in common with the world.

The philosophy of the beat generation can be stated in a few simple words: "I eat in this cold world, and I sleep in this cruel world, but I don't really *live* here."

And yet, if the farmer was too beat to grow and harvest grain, and the trucker was too beat to haul it away, and the brewer was too beat to fill the vats, and the bartender was too beat to serve his customers, the beat generation would have no beer to cry into.

No matter how sadly or soulfully it is phrased, the claim of being apart, detached and aloof is still an illusion. There is no way to live among people without being a part of human life.

No matter who we are, where we are born, how grand or insignificant we appear; no matter what our particular combination of nationality, race, color, sex health, I.Q., aptitudes or temperament, our presence on earth changes the status of the world by one new life, and it is not the same world it was before we came into it.

Our presence on earth means food for one more is needed, and someone must grow it; clothing for one more is needed, and someone must weave it; room for one more is needed, and someone must make it.

Almost every physical, mental, emotional and spiritual need we have must be satisfied by someone else—often a stranger we never meet. We must depend on someone to guard our national borders, and someone else to patrol our local streets. Someone must protect us from disease, someone else must teach us to read and write, another to play music, another to count numbers, another to see art, another to perform work. We have a need for friendship and someone else must be that friend. We have a need to love and be loved, and someone else must be beloved and lover.

Who must do these things for us? Other people?

No, not just other people. But other people disguised as farmers, sailors, clerks, teachers, soldiers, doctors, policemen, bakers, mechanics, parents, friends and sweethearts. And behind these disguises and human labels, other aloof, detached, isolated, unfathomable, dreaming, wondering, thinking, feeling, sensitive, individual, unique human beings, exactly like and completely different from ourselves.

Our human race is divided into more classifications than you can shake a stick at. Humans are labeled as men, women, white, colored, natives, foreigners, deists, atheists, cannibals and vegetarians. But there is no way to divide them up between those whose duty it is to understand and serve others, and those whose function is to be understood and served.

Whatever you ask of the world, of society, of your family—of other human beings—in the way of understanding, affection, kindness, assistance, tolerance and good will, you must be prepared to give in return. Even now. To your sister, to your mother and to me.

Do this and you will inherit a small miracle. As you begin to understand me and the others around you, you will find yourself being more understood. As you begin to discover and care for the world you live in, you will cease to be lost and a stranger in it. Now, as a boy, in your family and school world. Later, as a man, in the wide world of all mankind.

A FINAL
WORD

WHAT does the mysterious future hold in store for you?

Perhaps less that is mysterious and new than you now imagine.

At your age you have lived long enough to feel most of the emotions and participate in most of the experiences that life has to offer.

You know what it is to love and to hate. You have felt envy and compassion, jealousy and adoration. You have been vengeful and merciful, enjoyed freedom and struggled against restraint. You have been oppressed and you have exploited others. You know what it means to rebel and to obey, to be served honestly and to be deceived, to hope, to despair, to honor, to cheat, to laugh, to cry, to long for and to despise. You have known fear and fearlessness, confidence and doubt. You have been associated with birth, and you have been in the presence of death.

That's about all there is. And what has been will be, for the rest of your life. From now on, the newnesses in your life will be more those of position and title than of basically new relationships, situations and emotions.

Shakespeare wrote that all the world is a stage, and we are but players on it. That is not all. Except for set and costume changes, it is always the same play, with the same scenes endlessly repeated. The players change, but not the parts.

Today you play the part of an adolescent boy in the home. Your character and lines are new to you, the plot fresh. Tomorrow, against a different backdrop, with different props, you will play these same scenes again. But next time you will be cast as the father.

Unrehearsed and without a script, your child will return to your ear, in the jargon of his times, the same speeches you fling at mine, in the jargon of yours. And, as I once believed, and you believe, so will your child believe that it is the slangster, not merely his slang, that is something new under the sun.

The fact that you have experienced and reacted to most of your emotions does not mean you can always recognize which emotion is at work. You will probably dispute this. After all, who could be a better authority on how you feel than yourself? *Me?* Perhaps, sometimes. . . .

Human emotions are skilled, often sardonic players within the mind and body of the human actor. They delight in exchanging costumes and dialogues, one masquerading as the other to the confusion of their host. How often our emotions fool us, but no one else. Who else but the disappointed fox argues—and must believe—that the inaccessible grapes are sour?

A FINAL WORD   123

Pity sighs and sometimes convinces it is love. Envy conceals its pinched green face behind a sneer of contempt. Fear brags in a voice that perfectly mimics courage. Ignorance, muffled in the robes of superior knowledge, closes the mind's door to new ideas.

If I recognize emotions in you that have you fooled, it is not because I am smarter than you, but because I have seen the show before, I am familiar with the plot and I have seen the actors unmasked.

I will put it to you this way: Suppose you had someone in your car who had never seen an automobile before, and knew nothing of its operation. After taking that person for a drive, you might ask what made the car go, and he might reply, from observing you, that the gas pedal made the car go. When you pushed down on it, the car moved forward.

The gas pedal might be called the obvious reason why the car goes. But you and I know that unless the ignition is switched on, and the plugs are firing properly, and the carburetor is getting and vaporizing gasoline, and the transmission is engaged, and there are wheels and a dozen other necessary, hidden cooperations, the car will not move no matter how much you push down on the gas pedal.

As a teen-ager, you are pretty well acquainted with what I might call the dashboard emotions; the obvious switches and pedals and levers that seem to make the human machine go forward, back up, turn, change speeds, honk its horn and stop.

You know, at the dashboard level, how to operate your machine in traffic. But, emotionally, you still believe it is the obvious pedal that makes you go, and the obvious pedal that makes you stop. Unaware of crankshaft, pistons and cam, you hotly deny their existence, even while employing them.

My purpose, in these few letters to you, has been to take you under your own hood, and to acquaint you with more of the operating but unseen and unsuspected parts and functions that link your accelerator with your rear wheels, and your brake pedal with your brake drums.

If with my help you can learn to master your

machine, and negotiate safely the familiar routes of home, school and community, you will be able to proceed with confidence on any strange road in the world.